BIRD VIEWING AREAS

Wyoming Ecoregions

- Middle Rockies
- Wyoming Basin
- Wasatch and Uinta Mountains
- Northwestern Great Plains
- High Plains
- Southern Rockies

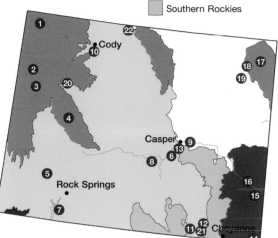

1. Yellowstone National Park
2. Grand Teton National Park
3. National Elk Refuge
4. Bridger-Teton National Forest
5. Seedskadee National Wildlife Refuge (NWR)
6. Audubon Center at Garden Creek
7. Flaming Gorge National Recreation Area
8. Pathfinder NWR
9. Edness K. Wilkins State Park
10. Draper Natural History Museum
11. Hutton Lake NWR
12. University of Wyoming Nature Center
13. Werner Wildlife Museum
14. Pine Bluffs Nature Area
15. Table Mountain Wildlife Habitat Management Area
16. Rawhide Wildlife Habitat Management Area
17. Black Hills National Forest
18. Devil's Tower National Monument
19. Keyhole State Park
20. National Bighorn Sheep Interpretive Center
21. Wyoming Children's Museum & Nature Center
22. Bighorn Canyon National Recreation Area

A POCKET NATURALIST® GUIDE

WYOMING BIRDS

A Folding Pocket Guide to Familiar Species

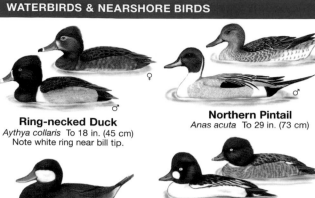

WYOMING BIRDS – A Folding Pocket Guide to Familiar Species

WATERFORD PRESS

WATERBIRDS & NEARSHORE BIRDS

Western Grebe
Aechmophorus occidentalis
To 25 in. (63 cm)

Pied-billed Grebe
Podilymbus podiceps
To 13 in. (33 cm)
Note banded white bill.

Eared Grebe
Podiceps nigricollis
To 14 in. (35 cm)
Note black neck and golden ear tufts.

Trumpeter Swan
Cygnus buccinator To 6 ft. (1.8 m)
Note stout black bill.

Canada Goose
Branta canadensis
To 45 in. (1.14 m)

Green-winged Teal
Anas crecca To 16 in. (40 cm) ♂

Blue-winged Teal
Spatula discors To 16 in. (40 cm) ♂

Mallard
Anas platyrhynchos To 28 in. (70 cm) ♂

Cinnamon Teal
Spatula cyanoptera To 17 in. (43 cm) ♂

Northern Shoveler
Spatula clypeata To 20 in. (50 cm) ♂
Named for its large spatulate bill.

American Wigeon
Mareca americana To 23 in. (58 cm) ♂

Gadwall
Mareca strepera To 23 in. (58 cm) ♂

Common Merganser
Mergus merganser To 27 in. (68 cm) ♂

WATERBIRDS & NEARSHORE BIRDS

Ring-necked Duck
Aythya collaris To 18 in. (45 cm)
Note white ring near bill tip.

Northern Pintail
Anas acuta To 29 in. (73 cm) ♂

Ruddy Duck
Oxyura jamaicensis To 16 in. (40 cm)
Note cocked tail.

Common Goldeneye
Bucephala clangula To 20 in. (50 cm) ♂

Canvasback
Aythya valisineria
To 2 ft. (60 cm)
Note sloping forehead and black bill.

Barrow's Goldeneye
Bucephala islandica To 20 in. (50 cm)
Male has a white facial crescent.

Killdeer
Charadrius vociferus
To 12 in. (30 cm)
Note two breast bands.

White-faced Ibis
Plegadis chihi
To 2 ft. (60 cm)

Great Blue Heron
Ardea herodias
To 4.5 ft. (1.4 m)

American Avocet
Recurvirostra americana
To 20 in. (50 cm)

Black-crowned Night-Heron
Nycticorax nycticorax
To 28 in. (70 cm)

Snowy Egret
Egretta thula
To 26 in. (65 cm)
Note black bill and yellow feet.

Willet
Tringa semipalmata
To 17 in. (43 cm)
Wings flash black-and-white in flight.

Double-crested Cormorant
Phalacrocorax auritus
To 3 ft. (90 cm)

WATERBIRDS & NEARSHORE BIRDS

American Coot
Fulica americana
To 16 in. (40 cm)

Spotted Sandpiper
Actitis macularius
To 8 in. (20 cm)
Breast is spotted.

Least Sandpiper
Calidris minutilla
To 6 in. (15 cm)

Sora
Porzana carolina
To 10 in. (25 cm)
Note stubby yellow bill and black patch on face and throat.

Sandhill Crane
Antigone canadensis
To 4 ft. (1.2 m)

Wilson's Snipe
Gallinago delicata
To 12 in. (30 cm)

Lesser Yellowlegs
Tringa flavipes
To 10 in. (25 cm)
Call is a 1-3 note whistle.

Greater Yellowlegs
Tringa melanoleuca
To 15 in. (38 cm)
Call is a 3-5 note whistle.

Long-billed Dowitcher
Limnodromus scolopaceus
To 12 in. (30 cm)
Breeding male has a rusty breast.

Franklin's Gull
Leucophaeus pipixcan
To 14 in. (35 cm)

American White Pelican
Pelecanus erythrorhynchos
To 5 ft. (1.5 m)

Ring-billed Gull
Larus delawarensis
To 20 in. (50 cm)
Bill has dark ring.

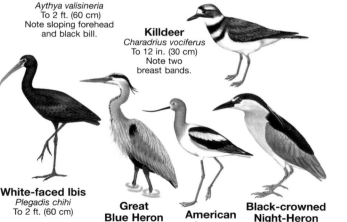

Forster's Tern
Sterna forsteri
To 15 in. (38 cm)
Note forked tail and white wing tips.

Black Tern
Chlidonias niger
To 10 in. (25 cm)
Head and belly are black.

California Gull
Larus californicus
To 23 in. (58 cm)
Note black and red spots on its bill.

UPLAND BIRDS

Ruffed Grouse
Bonasa umbellus
To 19 in. (48 cm)
Note black tail band.

Greater Sage-Grouse
Centrocercus urophasianus
To 30 in. (75 cm)

Sharp-tailed Grouse
Tympanuchus phasianellus
To 20 in. (50 cm)

Ring-necked Pheasant
Phasianus colchicus
To 3 ft. (90 cm)

Dusky Grouse
Dendragapus obscurus
To 21 in. (53 cm)

Wild Turkey
Meleagris gallopavo
To 4 ft. (1.2 m)

WOODPECKERS, DOVES, ETC.

Northern Flicker
Colaptes auratus
To 13 in. (33 cm)
Wing and tail linings are red.

Red-headed Woodpecker
Melanerpes erythrocephalus
To 10 in. (25 cm)

Downy Woodpecker
Dryobates pubescens
To 6 in. (15 cm)
The similar hairy woodpecker is larger and has a longer bill.

Red-naped Sapsucker
Sphyrapicus nuchalis
To 9 in. (23 cm)
Note red forehead and nape patches.

Rock Pigeon
Columba livia
To 13 in. (33 cm)

Mourning Dove
Zenaida macroura
To 13 in. (33 cm)

Common Nighthawk
Chordeiles minor
To 10 in. (25 cm)
Often hawks for insects around street lights.

Belted Kingfisher
Megaceryle alcyon
To 14 in. (35 cm)

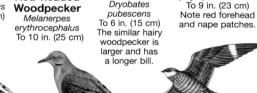

White-throated Swift
Aeronautes saxatalis
To 7 in. (18 cm)
Note thin pointed wings and white throat.

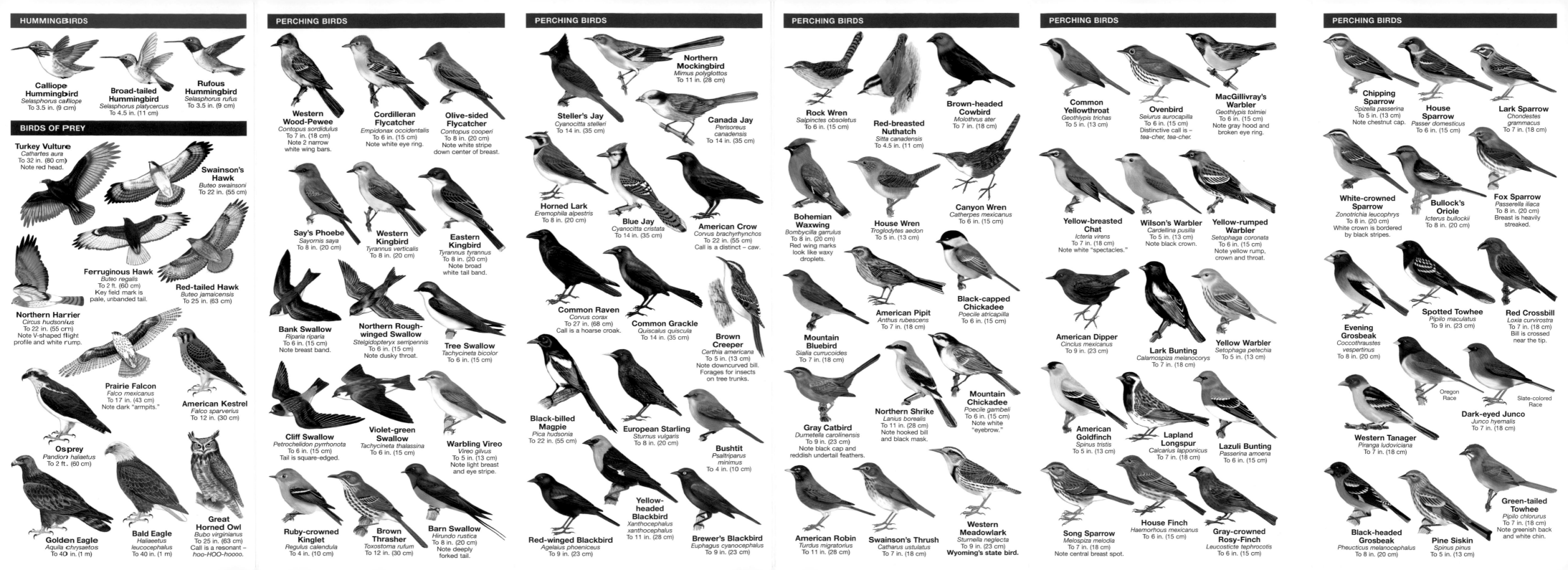

HUMMINGBIRDS

Calliope Hummingbird
Selasphorus calliope
To 3.5 in. (9 cm)

Broad-tailed Hummingbird
Selasphorus platycercus
To 4.5 in. (11 cm)

Rufous Hummingbird
Selasphorus rufus
To 3.5 in. (9 cm)

BIRDS OF PREY

Turkey Vulture
Cathartes aura
To 32 in. (80 cm)
Note red head.

Swainson's Hawk
Buteo swainsoni
To 22 in. (55 cm)

Ferruginous Hawk
Buteo regalis
To 2 ft. (60 cm)
Key field mark is pale, unbanded tail.

Red-tailed Hawk
Buteo jamaicensis
To 25 in. (63 cm)

Northern Harrier
Circus hudsonius
To 22 in. (55 cm)
Note V-shaped flight profile and white rump.

Prairie Falcon
Falco mexicanus
To 17 in. (43 cm)

American Kestrel
Falco sparverius
To 12 in. (30 cm)

Osprey
Pandion haliaetus
To 2 ft. (60 cm)

Golden Eagle
Aquila chrysaetos
To 40 in. (1 m)

Bald Eagle
Haliaeetus leucocephalus
To 40 in. (1 m)

Great Horned Owl
Bubo virginianus
To 25 in. (63 cm)
Call is a resonant – hoo-HOO-hooo.

PERCHING BIRDS

Western Wood-Pewee
Contopus sordidulus
To 7 in. (18 cm)
Note 2 narrow white wing bars.

Cordilleran Flycatcher
Empidonax occidentalis
To 6 in. (15 cm)
Note white eye ring.

Olive-sided Flycatcher
Contopus cooperi
To 8 in. (20 cm)
Note white stripe down center of breast.

Say's Phoebe
Sayornis saya
To 8 in. (20 cm)

Western Kingbird
Tyrannus verticalis
To 8 in. (20 cm)

Eastern Kingbird
Tyrannus tyrannus
To 8 in. (20 cm)
Note broad white tail band.

Bank Swallow
Riparia riparia
To 6 in. (15 cm)
Note breast band.

Northern Rough-winged Swallow
Stelgidopteryx serripennis
To 6 in. (15 cm)
Note dusky throat.

Tree Swallow
Tachycineta bicolor
To 6 in. (15 cm)

Cliff Swallow
Petrochelidon pyrrhonota
To 6 in. (15 cm)
Tail is square-edged.

Violet-green Swallow
Tachycineta thalassina
To 6 in. (15 cm)

Warbling Vireo
Vireo gilvus
To 5 in. (13 cm)
Note light breast and eye stripe.

Ruby-crowned Kinglet
Regulus calendula
To 4 in. (10 cm)

Brown Thrasher
Toxostoma rufum
To 12 in. (30 cm)

Barn Swallow
Hirundo rustica
To 8 in. (20 cm)
Note deeply forked tail.

PERCHING BIRDS

Northern Mockingbird
Mimus polyglottos
To 11 in. (28 cm)

Steller's Jay
Cyanocitta stelleri
To 14 in. (35 cm)

Canada Jay
Perisoreus canadensis
To 14 in. (35 cm)

Horned Lark
Eremophila alpestris
To 8 in. (20 cm)

Blue Jay
Cyanocitta cristata
To 14 in. (35 cm)

American Crow
Corvus brachyrhynchos
To 22 in. (55 cm)
Call is a distinct – caw.

Common Raven
Corvus corax
To 27 in. (68 cm)
Call is a hoarse croak.

Common Grackle
Quiscalus quiscula
To 14 in. (35 cm)

Brown Creeper
Certhia americana
To 5 in. (13 cm)
Note downcurved bill. Forages for insects on tree trunks.

Black-billed Magpie
Pica hudsonia
To 22 in. (55 cm)

European Starling
Sturnus vulgaris
To 8 in. (20 cm)

Bushtit
Psaltriparus minimus
To 4 in. (10 cm)

Red-winged Blackbird
Agelaius phoeniceus
To 9 in. (23 cm)

Yellow-headed Blackbird
Xanthocephalus xanthocephalus
To 11 in. (28 cm)

Brewer's Blackbird
Euphagus cyanocephalus
To 9 in. (23 cm)

PERCHING BIRDS

Rock Wren
Salpinctes obsoletus
To 6 in. (15 cm)

Red-breasted Nuthatch
Sitta canadensis
To 4.5 in. (11 cm)

Brown-headed Cowbird
Molothrus ater
To 7 in. (18 cm)

Bohemian Waxwing
Bombycilla garrulus
To 8 in. (20 cm)
Red wing marks look like waxy droplets.

House Wren
Troglodytes aedon
To 5 in. (13 cm)

Canyon Wren
Catherpes mexicanus
To 6 in. (15 cm)

American Pipit
Anthus rubescens
To 7 in. (18 cm)

Black-capped Chickadee
Poecile atricapilla
To 6 in. (15 cm)

Mountain Bluebird
Sialia currucoides
To 7 in. (18 cm)

Gray Catbird
Dumetella carolinensis
To 9 in. (23 cm)
Note black cap and reddish undertail feathers.

Northern Shrike
Lanius borealis
To 11 in. (28 cm)
Note hooked bill and black mask.

Mountain Chickadee
Poecile gambeli
To 6 in. (15 cm)
Note white "eyebrow."

American Robin
Turdus migratorius
To 11 in. (28 cm)

Swainson's Thrush
Catharus ustulatus
To 7 in. (18 cm)

Western Meadowlark
Sturnella neglecta
To 9 in. (23 cm)
Wyoming's state bird.

PERCHING BIRDS

Common Yellowthroat
Geothlypis trichas
To 5 in. (13 cm)

Ovenbird
Seiurus aurocapilla
To 6 in. (15 cm)
Distinctive call is – tea-cher, tea-cher.

MacGillivray's Warbler
Geothlypis tolmiei
To 6 in. (15 cm)
Note gray hood and broken eye ring.

Yellow-breasted Chat
Icteria virens
To 7 in. (18 cm)
Note white "spectacles."

Wilson's Warbler
Cardellina pusilla
To 5 in. (13 cm)
Note black crown.

Yellow-rumped Warbler
Setophaga coronata
To 6 in. (15 cm)
Note yellow rump, crown and throat.

American Dipper
Cinclus mexicanus
To 8 in. (20 cm)

Yellow Warbler
Setophaga petechia
To 5 in. (13 cm)

Lark Bunting
Calamospiza melanocorys
To 7 in. (18 cm)

American Goldfinch
Spinus tristis
To 5 in. (13 cm)

Lapland Longspur
Calcarius lapponicus
To 6 in. (15 cm)

Lazuli Bunting
Passerina amoena
To 6 in. (15 cm)

Song Sparrow
Melospiza melodia
To 7 in. (18 cm)
Note central breast spot.

House Finch
Haemorhous mexicanus
To 6 in. (15 cm)

Gray-crowned Rosy-Finch
Leucosticte tephrocotis
To 6 in. (15 cm)

PERCHING BIRDS

Chipping Sparrow
Spizella passerina
To 5 in. (13 cm)
Note chestnut cap.

House Sparrow
Passer domesticus
To 6 in. (15 cm)

Lark Sparrow
Chondestes grammacus
To 7 in. (18 cm)

White-crowned Sparrow
Zonotrichia leucophrys
To 8 in. (20 cm)
White crown is bordered by black stripes.

Bullock's Oriole
Icterus bullockii
To 8 in. (20 cm)

Fox Sparrow
Passerella iliaca
To 7 in. (18 cm)
Breast is heavily streaked.

Evening Grosbeak
Coccothraustes vespertinus
To 8 in. (20 cm)

Spotted Towhee
Pipilo maculatus
To 8 in. (20 cm)

Red Crossbill
Loxia curvirostra
To 7 in. (18 cm)
Bill is crossed near the tip.

Oregon Race

Slate-colored Race

Dark-eyed Junco
Junco hyemalis
To 7 in. (18 cm)

Western Tanager
Piranga ludoviciana
To 8 in. (20 cm)

Black-headed Grosbeak
Pheucticus melanocephalus
To 8 in. (20 cm)

Pine Siskin
Spinus pinus
To 5 in. (13 cm)

Green-tailed Towhee
Pipilo chlorurus
To 7 in. (18 cm)
Note greenish back and white chin.